Thank you for
coming out and supporting
my work!

— Paul Edward Cost

The Long Train of Chaos

Poems by Paul Edward Costa

Kung Fu Treachery Press

Rancho Cucamonga, CA

Copyright © Paul Edward Costa, 2019

First Edition 1 3 5 7 9 10 8 6 4 2

ISBN: 978-1-950380-55-8

LCCN: 2019947896

Design, edits and layout: John T. Keehan, Jr.

Cover and title page image: Shannon Moynagh

Author photo: Michelle Hillyard

Acknowledgments:

The author would like to thank the editors of these publications where some of the poems in this collection originally appeared:

Inside the Bell Jar: "Too Dark To See"
Bonk! Issue #2: "Vanity Of The Necromancer"
Alt-Minds Literary Magazine: "Your Head Will Collapse"
POST: "The Weak Who Justify The Strong" (Previously published
    as "Elixir of Ordnance")
The Eunoia Review: "The Fall," "Gethsemane"
The Gyroscope Review: "Magic Lamp Semantics"
Enduring Puberty Press, Issue #2: "The Shadows Ghosts Make"
Dryland_Lit: Los Angeles Underground Art and Writing #6:
    "I Met My Childhood Hero, And He Wants To Kill Me"
RE:AL Regarding Arts and Letters: "Once The Strings Are
    Cut, All Fall Down"
Brick Books: "Last Landline To The Source" (in audio format)

TABLE OF CONTENTS

Dedicated to Erich Gerner

CENTURY-CON

Booth #21
                              the last
at the convention of centuries
markets
crystal wares,
the clearest ever cut,
                    with a tag line:

The nightmares you bought on credit
                    burst from the closet

                    and the bill is due

while the preceding booths,
decorated like sacred shrines
          with a faint, saintly decorum,
advertise clean air
in the lands unscarred
by volcanic activity
     and the healing massage
offered by the tremors
of a rumbling earth stretching
                         to its limit.

FROM A SEEING-EYE SOCIOPATH

Do you think we don't have our fun
with the photos of the world
we transmit to your trusting brain?

Tear stains soak through the King's journal
as he sits alone in the throne room
among a council of black eyed Ministers.

Remember
that no mirrors exist
in the place where you live out your hallucinations

and know
that you'll never see a truthful sunrise
(though sunsets never lie),
you'll only rise early as a reaction
with all your actions a reversal of our every movement.

Wake up now
and open your mouth with a yawn

we must fall into sleep
and sigh backwards into dawn
then one step past it

before the past began

here the promise of rest

    can finally be fulfilled

        any night now I'm certain—

WAKE UP AND SMELL THE COSMIC TERROR

Imagine
going into the kitchen
        at 4:00am
            fluorescent lights
            still on
            over the backsplash
                and sink,
you need coffee
just a start
                to feel exhausted enough
                to fall back asleep.

A drawer rattles
so you open the drawer
    and see silver spoons suffering from seizures.

At first
in the spirit of communal love
        you consider cleaning them
        you consider smelting them
in a purifying fire
        before closing the drawer
        back into
    silence
and a cold truth—
                melted down

from bullets for werewolves,
the silver spoons possessed
by grand mal seizures
are already pure.

Now comes a moment of reflection
in the night kitchen's
monastic silence
where you realize

you've never owned a set of silver spoons.

AD POPULUM

I gathered courage
           left my front door
and hurled myself back
               as a screaming person crashed
               onto the asphalt sidewalk,
  breaking their bones
and tearing their flesh apart
        before a boy in shock
           a chalk white woman
              and a muscular man fell too,
onto a surface
where they didn't stay flattened for long
        thanks to a phenomenon
        by which they could heal and stand up
        like slack marionettes on suddenly tightened strings,
        fuelled by the rush of an impact
        so singularly painful
        it inspires divine Technicolor visions
        in anyone who joins the *building jumping* craze

but I've still never jumped,
      despite being made to attend cadet camps dedicated
                to the character building act
        of slamming into concrete at high speeds
      before re-entering a world
      newly welcoming
      and grown slightly grey.

DEPRESSION AT THE END OF TIME

Time moves along, and places
these places are its medium, its conductor
                                    necessary.

The places don't move
they only become vacant.

Within a few years after the final celebration
the place became emptier than it had before,
almost totally hollow:

the high-school an abandoned fortress,
the strip mall empty, closed stores, neon signs
desolate and dark, isolated in the suburbs
every single house existing in a time
                    before refreshing newness
                    but after the charmingly antique.

A waiting room disguised as an inferno.

During the day skies are only gray.

At night it always rains cold indifferent shards
of shattered glass.

So tired here
a dull atmospheric headache
eyes sore like organs rubbed against dry cement
                    in another empty day.

Comforting familiarity, always comfortable there,
reliability
no misery where expectations are dead
but this isn't the reality
                    objective or otherwise.

A brief sun, each day begins with splendor
the dark one not a snake or a seductive crown of fire
but boredom personified as King of the Monotones
                    (a surf band on the beach without waves
                    where water is washed thick with ash)

These demons, these damned fallen angels of activity
only march in after the morning establishment
of great expectations.

I think the old civilization called it depression,
the last survivors call it routine madness: the world
for lack of a better word stemming from a lacking glimpse
into eternity.

And who are they?

Some eat feces out of oyster shells
others fill a bottomless chest cavity forever
all supremely confident, obsessing over measured clouds
cold psychotic laughing and mad, on this basic drink:
2 parts syphilis, 1 part mercury
with preserving ice and a twist of wasted lives,
                    destroyed by the start
                    and starting many more.

Tough cockroaches scuttle in dry afterglow embers
of a nuclear holocaust. That's certain
but no longer comforting
to someone who has seen patterns in the explosions of light
and a face in the upwards stretch of a rising mushroom cloud.

TOO DARK TO SEE

A deep depression doesn't
          erase the world
  so much as it
slowly
suffocates the sun
until you think you've gone blind
    and feel an amalgamation with the dark.

A FLARE FROM THE BLUE DWARF STARS

The lights I chased,
the suns
 or AC bulbs,
detonated simultaneously,
demonstrating the true indifference
in their twinkling gaze,
   their long eyelash flames,
   their light particles washing over
my eternal
   crumbling form

                    (a year and a half after they went dark)

and I suffered a stroke
             that's lasted so long now
                    it's became my
personality.

FIGHTMUSICspells

He's addicted
to the atmosphere of the song,
          playing on repeat,
on the carpet,
in the basement,
sitting crouched and stoned
          still and poised to strike
          whatever crawls out from
the festering wound
of his habit-forming
          bittersweet thoughts;
     a broken parody of a pentagram
surrounds him:
               scattered pages,
     the pipe
                         the lighter
     and ground bud in a small pile
          on a book of plays by Harold Pinter
under the window slid open,
          on hard rain finally pounding the night's silence
into submission
                    like the galloping steel guitar
                    the subtle threat of the pattering drums
                    and the savage lyrics of a man who's
transcended the future

do to whatever crawls out from
the festering wound
of his habit-forming
    bittersweet thoughts
when he imagines himself as a dead dry sycamore:
        a system of thoughts
      beaten into a dense
      clusterofINSTINCT*

*a man who's scrubbed out the baptism of consciousness
    with steel wool
and become a vessel for nature's eviscerating wisdom,
    a power only an aphrodisiac
      for an ego always warped to the brink
        of redefinition
          by an atmosphere of addictive,
            seductive submission
        until the blackout
          brings down electric dreams…

The song playing on repeat fades
      out for the last time
        and the hard rain softens

AFTER THE GRID

And while noir rain pounds down
on this dim house
with only a secret front door leading in
(behind a warehouse
            down a flight of unused stairs)
awake in the kitchen,
our radio plays static,
smoke billows across the TV's black image,
and I'm singing gentle songs—
the kind you sing
burning out from amphetamines
                        at dawn
after a power surge
through the outlet where you've plugged yourself in
fries you in a slow burn for months
with low crackling
            buzzing currents
                        of electricity

THE AGE OF REASON'S RAIN DANCE

Salvation will come
to those
who clamp jumper cables
      linked to a car battery
      onto Fate's
      empty testicles,
re-enacting
      Ben Franklin's
      key, kite,
   and lightening experiment,
forcing
      Fate's utterance
      of the prayer hidden past
  reason,
      whose meaning changes
      if it isn't screamed out in agony
      from Fate's scorched, smouldering,
        and smoking corpse,
      keeping its head thrown back
      jaw open,
      about to laugh
      like the hell of a delayed sneeze
    on a field beneath the invoked storm,
commanding
      fear in the population
      who

on holiday

observe travelling torturers seeking salvation

from Fate

whose flesh feels like dried out timber

because convulsions induced

by electrocution

make a piss-poor rain dance

while travelers watch the fusion of

thought out will and primal nature

with love in their hearts

from a safe distance.

SUPERVILLAIN ORIGINS: THE GRANDMASTER

The serum through the syringe
    stopper pushed down
            through the glistening pupil,
            into the highway veins of bloodshot eyes

  as cells morph
    into meta-cells
                advanced
                and gifted
with mastery over their predecessors...

until he rises
from the incubation tank
and the bio lab,
                as fruits filled with virtuous compassion
                and pits of torment
                die on synthetic vines

but no hunger pains him
                he doesn't mind,
walking alone,
        contented
into the populated world
                bustling cities
                screaming cicada woods,
there is nature to advance,

       to alter

and soft

   moving statues

     to imbue with life

         who he'll bring closer to the core.

THE MAN WHO ESCAPED AN LSD TESTING FACILITY

He walks
across the empty windswept plains
like a man
      on his own secret
            obscure mission.
A full,
     coarse beard
      and a military cap
hide his beady black
charcoal eyes.

THE VANITY OF THE NECROMANCER

The skulls pass from him like eggs and he fertilizes them in the green fire. Stargazing in a celestial storm seared his retinal wall with hell's sky vomiting fire onto blasted landscapes. His crimson eyes see through the dreams floating in burning clouds and he waits to knight you with his scythe. The skulls crawl gratefully over the black ground towards the flames that will nurture them while they pray for disintegration.

SERENITY IN SILVER

He clicks the hammer into place
on his celestial revolver made of silver,
in the pursuit of dreams,
executing them when he captures their mystic throats
beneath his boot
with a double tap to the heart
and one shot to the mind
on cloud dusted, half seen
desolate highways of distant heaven.

WHEN THE CRADLE ROCKS AFTER THE HAND HAS BEEN SEVERED

I fell silent
when I saw the face
across from my own
form the solemn grimace
     and far-away stare
it's said we take on
in the instant before fully committing
to the vague hieroglyphs of a psychopath
        or the reality of a private utopia
   collapsing
into violent contradictions.

THEY TOOK A WALK THROUGH THE ANCIENT GALLERY

Shuffling slowly through the cavernous art gallery,
they're walking in small disjointed groups,
        heads bowed so low their necks snap,
            as spinal bones emerge fractured and sharp
        with spinal fluid flowing
onto polished floors, making them slick
        and delicately encouraging an ancient fall.

Brush strokes on works of art never change
but with walls of silence collapsing in
off physical walls of gun metal plaster,
the farther they march
the more every painted smile becomes a sneer,
making works celebrating the eternal spirit
glow with menace.

A long drone grows from a small crack
in the farthest gallery wall, a promise
belching out dust filled mist
covering the room in a fine film
making almost everyone's eyes squint into a narrow vision
        while some step back
            to see a billion specs of dust emerge at once
        around a phoenix of elegant filth risen from everything.

FEARING YOUR SHADOW AT NIGHTFALL

The city gave birth to that which engulfs it in flames
    with a stream of liquid fire raining down from sunset
        and towers rising like teeth towards the setting blood moon,
but worst of all,
their ash symbols mark the shells of our buildings
while they construct charred black structures in their image

                    as fate closes her window's shutters,

and while I desperately seek sanctuary,
        I still fear any force with the power to endure.

THE CHANTING WALL

I hurled my body against the cinderblock
                                    wall,
falling down face-first to the bone covered
                                    ground
each time my textbook of subatomic
                                    physics
promised enough room between atoms for a
                                    universe
but science doesn't move me alone because the
                                    arts
appeared as a cry I heard from the wall after I
                                    fell
when I shouted out in shock and despair at my
                                    limit,
and figured the cry came from my soul on the other
                                    side
of the wall imprisoning dreamers while killing off
                                    amnesiacs
forever until the wall's engineers are granted their
                                    hypothesis
when we transcend the wall both physically and
                                    psychologically

                    at
                        the

same

time.

Countless epigraphs to their efforts sit etched into the wall's

face,

mocking broken bodies in the

dust.

PERSISTENCE #9

Evenly smoothed concrete makes the wall
no end to the left the right or above
in our limited vision
of un-chipped gray stained by blood.

The man disappears from sight
then comes back running
            into the wall again,
        disappears from sight
then comes back running
(wearing a gold medal of honour)
            into the wall again,
        disappears from sight
then comes back running
(wearing the coloured pants of a clown)
            into the wall again,
and retreats,
decorated with a purple heart squirting water:
distinguished becoming ridiculous,
and then a ridiculous parody of distinguished
before knowing the madness
                    you don't know,
                    have never known
not here—

YOUR HEAD WILL COLLAPSE

No one
loses
    their mind;
they simply
open the door
    to their skull
and reveal
    the abandoned orphanage
and the haunted cities
inside.

ADRENAL INFLATION

They said he felt too much
            with too much sensitivity,
        that he'd only survive
by transmuting
            epinephrine
                    into
                            valium,
            spectacle
                    into
                            routine,
and after countless cycles of
                    meditation and reflection,
                    medication and talk therapy,
he made the mistake of thinking
he'd mastered his heart rate
after three and a half hours of uninterrupted pornography.

THE PUNK SAGE'S WISDOM

I find
that the best meditation
for living in the moment
            through a detachment from time
is to hide your hand
beneath your clothing
                casually
as if to scratch
            an itch
and raise your middle finger
when your triggers trap you
                and wrap you
in a cosmic swaddle of claustrophobia.

They'll have no idea
how close they stand
to the truth they fear.

THE WEAK WHO JUSTIFY THE STRONG

The second of my two daily pills
fell to the floor
where its capsule cracked
in half,
seventy-five milligrams
setting fire to the old apartment
where you used to live
and every former tenant
filled with nostalgia's audacity

since a group's lamentation
is never really a lament

where every step taken
lands next to a framed mirror
labelled as a painting
so *narcissism* simply becomes
art appreciation
while the stumbling blind can be openly mocked
as barbarians

and are.

NOTHING TO BE DONE

With their eyes hanging
                    dislodged
      at the ends of their stalks
            dangling
      and bouncing against their
cheeks
they laughed truly
with true savagery,
swinging their heads back and
forth
             right and
left
horizontally,
       (never up or down)
whipping their eyes around their heads
       like a failed game of paddle-ball
       like tetherballs on ropes attached
to poles grown sentient and self-aware
playing by themselves after transcending the need for
players
      because
           what else could they do?

MEDITATION ON RAGE

His hands on the desk, and the desk spins with him
in trembling delirium

before both hands bring their shaking tempests up
and the pen falls to the work surface with a clatter.

Bulging tendons around flexing white knuckles,
an attempt to grasp what's slipped away.

Here static stillness buzzes with more potential energy
than that expended by the physical release of ordinary anger.

Eyes close.

In the darkness of perception, a non-linear film plays
where razor thoughts float as islands in the void.

Flashes of twisted fantasy: a face swollen black and blue
is slammed into cement again, led by the belt around it

and the hands with bulging tendons
            around flexing white knuckles.

Fade out to white and in again. A mouth of broken teeth
mumbles apologies that tumble in an arsenic cascade
of sweet sought after nectar.

Breathe. Just breathe heavy and deep now.
Greet the world with open eyes and a kindness so rehearsed,
its surface glimmers with perfectly warm authenticity.

ARCHMIEDES' BLOODBATH

After the dirt
     and energy displaced by our conflict
settled,
the wrathful heat waves
   we held in reserve
cooked them into feverish dreams
         of set winners and losers
          when, in the end,
    there's only
     those who can stay in the castle's courtyard
   and those who are banished to the frontier
        by fading ink on a treaty
           promising empathy
        between specks shrinking into the distance
and lights from the top floor
   of a fortified tower.

IF ACTAEON WAS AN ATHEIST

I've never felt the touch of god
           or the presence of the lord,
           or sensed a spirit in the static
           of a séance caught on cassette;
By now,
I've long since abandoned the ritual
           of checking closets before bed
and sometimes
I'll even stay in a basement consumed by blackness,
           near the door of an open cellar,
           just to test my belief in the emptiness
           of the void where I stand,
but that doesn't mean
    I've never seen demons
        possess a personality,

because a familiar voice called me
           with calm reason to a childhood place,
           warping into a song of unhinged hatred
           when it had me alone,

because I've felt the full weight
           of unprocessed pain passing onto my shoulders,

and seen Dr. Jekyll transform into Hyde
           before my very eyes.

A SOCRATIC DARE

Show me the man
    who's mastered himself
    who still sees reality as his own creation
        chance as a chant of the unworthy
        and silence as approval
      from a rocking chair surrounded by eggshells
          where, if left too long,
          he begins thinking
          that careful walking on tiptoes
          is a beautiful dance...

Show me,
    please...
I'll wait.

I'VE SEEN YOUR FACE BEFORE, MY FRIEND

Someone facing defeat
    might pull a knife out of their boot
      or a pin out of a grenade
      as a desperate last act
    but that's nothing
  than a feud
stripped to its nucleus;

what's hazardous
    is every overthrown oppressor finally facing the abyss
        of their empty conscience
who *Only wants to talk*
because although I've never heard what's been said
when they do
    I've seen those who've been so persuaded
    come within an inch of leaving hell's gates
  before turning around
  and walking back
into caverns filled
with the sulfuric smoke of vague sentences
    containing everything

so I've lit the candles on this birthday cake
with a saw inside for cutting your chains
and wax on top for plugging your ears
    before you try to escape.

IS THIS TO BE AN EMPTHY TEST?

If you can nod in polite agreement
      when I claim that *Of course kerosene cures flames,*
      then congratulations,
   for you'll have finally traded
the compassion of your vulnerable youth
            for the sociopathic perspective
                  reaching the end of the line requires
                        from which
      a life's endless descent
through hell's pandemonium
looks like a fictional sitcom
showing self-sabotaging,
      unsympathetic characters
            so you never need to feel
            the deep cuts that are made
            by caring's surgical blades.

THE FALL

Descending down
        the cliff's rocky
                spiral path
tighter until in one place
I spin
becoming trapped in a claustrophobic crevice
the anesthesiologist fills with
             gas.
Count backwards from forty
           in order
                 to fall into yourself
still spiralling
until the temperature falls
and the inferno stops
under a reign of stillness and ice
the fires becoming icicles risen from Tartarus.

The Damned arriving frequently
            and en mass
               hell so full
  its putrid landscape
causes exactly as much pain
as its bureaucratic pandemonium.

On grainy black and white security monitors
whispers of white souls rush through the abyss,

it's torturers, receptionists, and administrators
just outside cavernous chambers of agony
feel drafts of cold chilling their bones blurring the line
between patient and doctor, sufferer and Devil.

GETHSEMANE

When I first went there
my feet carried me to the door of the mansion
I couldn't help it.
I knocked
      and Lucifer opened the door,
      his thin, pale, delicate hand emerged
      from black robes,
      grabbed me
      pulled
         me
            inside,
      and flayed my flesh ten thousand times
                ten thousand ways
as slight variations made each strike from Lucifer's claws
    unique.

The last time I went there
I walked the path leading to the door of the mansion
purely by my own choice.
I knocked
      and Lucifer opened the door
      in a black, three piece, double breasted suit
      with a glass of eighteen-year-old scotch in one hand
      saying nothing before turning around
      and walking towards the study
            to set out our clear chess pieces

into a shifting glass garden of logic.
Lucifer sat, slouched, and played an opening move.
I took my place, forced a half smile,
and accepted the noble challenge
of playing through to an endgame
against an invulnerable King.

My sweat was like great drops of blood falling
down upon the ground.

THE GASLAMP IN THE DEMON'S RIGHT HAND

One day,
a friar emerged
alongside the Demon
 who found souls deflecting
 his savage expressions
 and caustic decrees
  by dismissing him in their minds
 as just another monster
from the depths
  not of their concern,
  or of their kind,
but with a holy man nearby
 weeping and wailing about the Demon's
   fall from grace,
  his rocky path,
  and the respect
 his *wounded genius* deserves,
they tie barbed wire about their thighs
 to atone for *denying that poor,*
  dark prince his purpose,
  and for *not bowing to a leader with enough charisma*
  *to make souls walk **into** the fire,*
as anyone able to resist that voice
 is exiled to a place
 where they gather

and plan the friar's demise,
  hoping his face warps into an inhuman shape
  when they hold him under saltwater waves.

AND / OR PLAGUE

She was
the most honest Doctor
        I ever knew,
no
final cures
or
eradications
came out of her practice's lab.

Sometimes
        at night
she wept in uncontrollable
        lamentation
for humanity
        withering
before the materialized silence
        the great leveler,

like her patient
cured of leukemia
who
fell into blackest depression
        at its remission
        as the retreat
of her identity's
                unique
                organic tension
slackened and undefined her features.

All she could do
was consider the effect
        of the unchecked silence,
                    shudder
and smear another smudge of spackle
on the crumbling dam
                of a deep collective lake.

She could not
in good conscience
give a *clean* bill of health
        to anyone,
        to everyone
standing
            before the materialized silence
                the great leveler

The patients didn't hear
                the roar
of silence's ever-scream
but felt
its psychosomatic ramifications
so she affixed
        a suffix
to every diagnosis she gave,
that the patient
suffered from
-insert affliction here-
                and/or plague.

AMERICANA MELTING

Eleanor sits in the Glass Falls Diner
an atmosphere of coffee from white porcelain cups
when the waitress drops one to the checkered floor
she'll pick it up without spilling a drop
while no one flinches, but they'll flicker.
Outside the sky fades violet with bright stars
and Eleanor looks calm, perfectly stable,
hands folded on the Formica table,
wondering about passionate escape
and wishing for amnesia on a faraway beach.

HER INCIDENTAL COLLAPSE

A year forced to its crisis in her room
            above glittering Las Vegas
shattered mirrors falling, bloody fractured fists their center
    leftover cocaine sprinkled
on old vodka bottles arranged like jewels.

She screams long and in reverse, arriving at fear's birth:

    a slight shift of the Black King slumped asleep on his throne

I HAVE THE BEST SAFE WORD

The Dominatrix
        faced her fidgeting client
                before their first session,
            and while zipping up her mask
                            she asked
                which safe word he'd selected;
she said
        PUKE
        is popular for being pretty repulsive
while many choose
                CURDLED
                to conjure the scent of expired milk
although others use
                STROODLE
                to sink a sensual mood
but her client,
        confused,
        only asked why a simple
                        NO
                        wouldn't suffice instead,
    stunning her into silence
                as she discarded her mask,
                    shocked by a rare specimen of innocence
                    somehow still unscathed
                        by twisted,
                            weaponized words.

MAGIC LAMP SEMANTICS

You'll never hear sentences
            so elaborately
            and carefully constructed
as the wishes now made to genies,
so airtight
            (filled with dashes and semi-colons)
that they're immune to any cruel,
                        ironic,
                        Twilight Zone interpretations,
leaving the occupants of magic lamps
            brooding behind folded arms,
nostalgic for an era
            when well-wishers spoke carelessly,
            so genies could openly engage
            in the malevolent manipulations
                reserved for the gods.

THEIR SHADOWS RISE UP IN REVOLT

In the kingdoms
of the disturbed
no such thing exists
as
        forgiveness;
only reminders and remembrance remain
with no statute of limitations.

A refugee recently arrived
from those regions.
He had the longest memory ever recorded
and slouched from the weight of 10,000 mutated,
                invisible recollections
           clinging heavily to every limb.

He said
      We abolished our regular purge of memory
      and forgot the humbling
      never touched bottom of the mind's cup.

      Dreaming of a fantasy skyline,
      we aimed our foresight far past
      the diamond rim
            of the mind's cup.

Now the sewers of psychosis overflow

as our shadows rise up in revolt.

At the welcoming ball
in his honour
he danced
      like a horse
      with its rider slumped over dead in the saddle.

THE SHADOWS GHOSTS MAKE

The ghosts haunted me since I was a child
but
since I never learned the word for
corporeal phantom
they only thought
that I diligently practiced
the art of
polite conversation

though the strange thing
is that I somehow did improve my communication
by staring through the translucent forms
of whoever I spoke with

while the downside became seeing
the hook handed shadows
rising behind them

who I didn't think could hurt me
but who I feared might tear apart the ghosts I saw,
my only company,
although they had no ears
with which to collect the empathetic sounds
of my frantic voice.

EITHER A BEAST OR A GOD

The violence of the beast
    didn't break me as completely
        as the sight of it casually slouching away,
        admiring bellflowers,
        and summoning a portal back to its realm.

The sharp crack of its tail left swollen cuts
that healed faster than the sting
        the lack of recognition on its face
        made in my mind
when I tracked it down and woke it up
    before sending it back into the shadows
    grown around me like a black cloak
        blocking out
        concussions of darkness
    while somehow still letting through
  songs sung in secret
by the dead beast's human disciples.

I MET MY CHILDHOOD HERO, AND HE WANTS
TO KILL ME

I met the Emperor only once,
          looked in his eyes
      and saw a familiar
                wrathful lunacy
in place of
              divine love,
unless cupid constructed his compound bow
          for the purpose of disfiguring god's image,
                        his template
                  when anointing rulers of the earth.

In him
the new courtiers saw
                a stoic figure
                dignifying the indifference
                      of the
      disconnected

on the throne where the old ministers saw
                              the still-born
corpse of an idea.

WHAT DID THE PEN SAY TO THE SWORD?

Our governor gave orders
        to bind the prisoners' feet,
        toss them down the mountainside
    and pull them up over thorny vines
            again and again till tender and torn
            so they'll heal with thick scabs
            on the soft undersides of their psyches

and yet the visiting Empress,
            bearing witness
                    reacts with revulsion
saying
        Outlaw what you seek to destroy
        and you'll spend every second smothering
                        the very principle of resistance

        render it rude, however
        and they'll tear what's forbidden
                out of each other all on their own

as your officers unruffled uniforms
    still attract unyielding affection,
as the clean soles of their boots
    still calm the faces on which they stomp
            with an aroma of fresh rubber like the smell of a new car.

ONCE THE STRINGS ARE CUT, ALL FALL DOWN

After a while,
I stopped turning on the lights
when I got home at night;
the darkness felt
                familiar,
like an old blanket.
I knew what sat there in the shadows
                and where.

In the sudden blackout
a woman down the hall
                managed to hit all the speed dial contacts
                        on her cell phone at once,
awakening a dissonant surge of voices
who trip the breaker of her thoughts,

but my night
like a nightmare
has no bottom
    no nadir,
sight gives way to
                blindness,
sound gives way to
                deafness,
until absence without limit
                arrives fashionably late

just to mock
            the calls of a hopeful search party.

In the vacuous eternity,
those versed in chaos's braille
navigate the void between stars
                    by feeling
                            nothing.

In the vacuous eternity,
those versed in sense's warm logic
huddle like children
            on lunar outposts,
delicately singing the alphabet aloud

in the vacuous eternity:

THE AUDIOPHILE'S THIRD EAR

The records are blank
with no rings cut
    into black vinyl
and playing them
    never triggers
      a mass of shrieking harmonics
        time might transpose into a symphony
          —only silence
        quietly accompanied
      by just
      the slightest static fuzz,
      popping and crackling occasionally
    to prove
    beyond a shadow of a doubt
that this vacuum was made
    this nothing is real
      (a real abyss has gravity)

and some mind,
    somewhere
conceived its creation.

THE LAST LANDLINE TO THE SOURCE

You have a collect prayer
           from *beneath the foundation*
will you accept its charges?

****

Nothing,
           your power is immense
           and so
Logic,
       your most faithful disciple
       in a letter from him to our forgotten country
       suggested I pray to you
    a suggestion
               I soberly accept.

No idealist myself,
           I'll not suggest salvation,
           I know your inventory
doesn't match
               the promise of your cold call advertising,
but grace,
       that
       I beg you to send
                   to those perpetually dying

in locked rooms
with no emergency services
     on the speed dials of their disconnected phones.
Vortices of paradox
warp the images visible
   in the eyepieces
   of the telescopes they've turned inwards;
many blurs
of
   inherent nature
   battling
   learned thought
          or
            perfect sanity
            resisting
            a slide into madness
reshape their identities
     into personified wounds
replacing their bodies
   with substantial pain
on a molecular level.

You,
unseen in the back
but still reeking through the crowd
please, do not in jest
       suggest a cheap vaudeville show
       for healing a warped soul,
a false imitation

                    of an authentic desire's dream
does nothing
            to displace the pressure
            of the imp crouched on your chest
                        grinning in your face
and only lets it sit more heavily
            on an empty chest cavity
            with no limit to the volume of its void.

Give them
            the tools to
                        endure
and a telescopic lens
            powerful enough
                        to view that victory.

IT'S NICE TO SEE AN END TO THE LONG TRAIN OF CHAOS

The long train of chaos
                    is coming to an end
but
    I have no problem
                    re-opening its rearmost baggage car
once more
        if need be,
to access a power
that can tear up its tracks
                        into
                        twisted metal sculptures,
                        straining to maintain a defiance of gravity.

            Its rail line cut a straight path to the edge of land
                but all who followed its clear promise
            found themselves gradually turning
        and circling back over the same places again,
                back over the tracks
                    —once secured with spikes to the earth—
warping
        into steel trees haunted by dryads
                        praising the sun.

POST-SCRIPT

So remember
if you see me again
to say a prayer,
       make peace with your sins,
    and square yourself with the times
you sold fear as the only morality
    to souls falling into shock
                   when the black planet rose
                        in place of the sun
because it'll mean I've started down a road
         I won't be following back.

Paul Edward Costa is a writer, spoken word artist, teacher, and the 2019-2021 Poet Laureate for the City of Mississauga. He has featured at many poetry reading series in the Greater Toronto Area and has published over 60 poems, stories, and articles in literary journals such as *Bewildering Stories, Lucent Dreaming Magazine, Entropy Magazine, Gyroscope Review, POST-, and Alt-Minds Literary Magazine.* His novella, *Dark Magic on the Edge of Town,* was put out in 2017 with the hybrid publisher Paperback-Press. He curates/hosts the YTGA Open Mic Series at Studio.89, has co-organized/hosted the Mississauga Arts Council's Verses Out Loud Poetry Series, and has won the Mississauga Arts Council's 2019 MARTY Award for Emerging Literary Arts.

BLACK DRAGON POETRY SOCIETY

CERTIFIED AND APPROVED

CPSIA information can be obtained
at www.ICGtesting.com
Printed in the USA
LVHW110110111019
633870LV00001B/35/P